TABLE OF CONTENTS

Workbook Answers

Chapter 1 - Whole Numbers

Pg 6

1.

1	5	6	3	2	7	8	2
Ten Millions	Millions	Hundred Thousands	Ten Thousands	Thousands	Hundreds	Tens	Ones

2.

2	4	8	7	9	3	6	0
Ten Millions	Millions	Hundred Thousands	Ten Thousands	Thousands	Hundreds	Tens	Ones

3.

6	2	1	5	8	5	2	4
Ten Millions	Millions	Hundred Thousands	Ten Thousands	Thousands	Hundreds	Tens	Ones

4.

3	0	6	7	1	2	3	4
Ten Millions	Millions	Hundred Thousands	Ten Thousands	Thousands	Hundreds	Tens	Ones

5.

5	2	1	9	7	3	0	5
Ten Millions	Millions	Hundred Thousands	Ten Thousands	Thousands	Hundreds	Tens	Ones

6.

8	3	4	9	8	1	4	7
Ten Millions	Millions	Hundred Thousands	Ten Thousands	Thousands	Hundreds	Tens	Ones

Pg 7

7	4	8	4	2	2	7	1	9
Hundred Millions	Ten Millions	Millions	Hundred Thousands	Ten Thousands	Thousands	Hundreds	Tens	Ones

1.

3	2	9	6	0	8	1	1	4
Hundred Millions	Ten Millions	Millions	Hundred Thousands	Ten Thousands	Thousands	Hundreds	Tens	Ones

2.

1	2	4	3	7	5	2	7	7
Hundred Millions	Ten Millions	Millions	Hundred Thousands	Ten Thousands	Thousands	Hundreds	Tens	Ones

3.

7	4	1	5	8	8	3	7	9
Hundred Millions	Ten Millions	Millions	Hundred Thousands	Ten Thousands	Thousands	Hundreds	Tens	Ones

4.

5	0	4	2	6	7	3	3	2
Hundred Millions	Ten Millions	Millions	Hundred Thousands	Ten Thousands	Thousands	Hundreds	Tens	Ones

5.

9	7	2	1	1	4	0	8	9
Hundred Millions	Ten Millions	Millions	Hundred Thousands	Ten Thousands	Thousands	Hundreds	Tens	Ones

6.

Pg 8		Pg 9		Pg 10	
No.	Answer	No.	Answer	No.	Answer
1	3,000	1	24,453	1	900 + 400 = 1,300
2	9,000	2	55,718	2	500 + 500 = 1,000
3	1,000	3	19,554	3	100 + 600 = 700
4	8,000	4	28,132	4	400 + 700 = 1,100
5	3,000	5	12,966	5	900 - 500 = 400
6	4,000	6	93,359	6	800 - 200 = 600
7	6,000	7	96,591	7	600 - 500 = 100
8	8,000	8	56,772	8	400 - 200 = 200
9	6,000	9	83,297		
10	2,000	10	27,915		
11	40,000	11	35,212		
12	20,000	12	62,689		
13	90,000	13	49,212		
14	60,000	14	79,359		
15	70,000	15	93,756		
16	80,000	16	41,328		
17	30,000	17	43,957		
18	40,000	18	14,161		
19	20,000	19	93,564		
20	50,000	20	39,817		
21	300,000				
22	600,000				
23	200,000				
24	500,000				
25	200,000				
26	300,000				
27	900,000				
28	600,000				
29	800,000				
30	100,000				

Pg 11		Pg 12		Pg 13	
No.	Answer	No.	Answer	No.	Answer
1	6,000 + 4,000 = 10,000	1	1,225	1	6,515
2	5,000 + 1,000 = 6,000	2	1,024	2	12,834
3	9,000 + 7,000 = 16,000	3	1,580	3	12,670
4	5,000 + 5,000 = 10,000	4	742	4	11,229
5	3,000 + 6,000 = 9,000	5	1,261	5	16,342
6	8,000 + 7,000 = 15,000	6	1,111	6	8,877
7	2,000 + 5,000 = 7,000	7	1,353	7	5,300
8	4,000 + 5,000 = 9,000	8	1,632	8	11,866
9	9,000 + 500 = 9,500	9	1,236	9	13,940
10	4,000 - 2,000 = 2,000	10	1,430	10	9,715
11	9,000 - 5,000 = 4,000			11	15,009
12	7,000 - 6,000 = 1,000			12	5,461
13	5,000 - 3,000 = 2,000			13	4,177
14	9,000 - 8,000 = 1,000			14	15,408
15	4,000 - 2,000 = 2,000			15	13,512
16	4,000 - 800 = 3,200			16	24,745
17	6,000 - 2,000 = 4,000			17	10,693
18	8,000 - 6,000 = 2,000			18	14,319
				19	14,792
				20	14,112

Pg 14		Pg 15		Pg 16	
No.	Answer	No.	Answer	No.	Answer
1	23,795	1	104,654	1	596,052
2	16,340	2	188,944	2	977,698
3	16,891	3	144,072	3	1,160,308
4	23,486	4	189,476	4	1,097,102
5	18,748	5	104,323	5	1,089,063
6	22,475	6	103,894	6	1,283,759
7	20,531	7	156,084	7	1,336,765
8	13,385	8	140,874	8	845,509
9	13,938	9	184,913	9	1,051,175
10	19,146	10	147,781	10	1,085,891
11	17,264	11	57,012	11	1,975,054
12	17,039	12	183,425	12	841,668
13	16,951	13	131,969	13	1,410,112
14	14,558	14	101,039	14	1,518,639
15	22,189	15	184,161	15	2,240,839
16	14,766	16	115,576	16	720,411
17	21,953	17	83,250	17	1,776,777
18	13,765	18	68,871	18	1,577,184
19	8,331	19	174,540	19	1,304,447
20	18,795	20	264,261	20	1,662,926

Pg 17		Pg 18		Pg 19	
No.	Answer	No.	Answer	No.	Answer
1	12,052,629	1	443	1	1,112
2	7,888,122	2	452	2	1,111
3	17,265,467	3	143	3	3,781
4	21,709,039	4	284	4	2,779
5	14,622,984	5	539	5	1,756
6	11,129,457	6	118	6	6,487
7	19,771,741	7	861	7	7,511
8	17,143,156	8	451	8	2,264
9	10,170,485	9	252	9	524
10	14,603,355	10	129	10	5,685
11	23,268,932	11	291	11	327
12	13,589,274	12	450	12	2,047
13	15,296,451	13	288	13	4,635
14	17,280,455	14	457	14	2,059
15	12,562,642	15	432	15	5,475
16	15,576,391			16	2,889
17	15,540,467			17	1,454
18	15,214,301			18	916
19	22,608,631			19	2,755
20	20,429,648			20	2,747

Pg 20		Pg 21		Pg 22	
No.	Answer	No.	Answer	No.	Answer
1	2,786	1	131,482	1	592,288
2	25,038	2	507,851	2	1,409,294
3	21,376	3	277,758	3	5,730,630
4	36,508	4	34,013	4	2,437,389
5	20,756	5	778,375	5	2,113,834
6	16,804	6	191,436	6	5,220,339
7	20,507	7	411,246	7	7,314,169
8	4,557	8	352,113	8	2,876,907
9	37,509	9	221,963	9	3,135,552
10	38,809	10	232,179	10	5,127,660
11	18,499	11	47,078	11	1,801,944
12	26,055	12	181,244	12	4,683,052
13	15,864	13	426,781	13	3,125,607
14	43,464	14	151,044	14	4,587,627
15	45,132	15	374,747	15	3,670,658
16	46,172	16	96,861	16	3,371,113
17	18,489	17	189,668	17	6,478,871
18	21,529	18	412,017	18	2,359,169
19	57,435	19	199,681	19	3,467,162
20	76,939	20	619,306	20	2,282,335

Pg 23	
No.	Answer
1	13,138,506
2	30,680,207
3	22,547,298
4	35,657,655
5	7,593,206
6	46,473,155
7	55,559,777
8	89,277,747
9	34,798,707
10	19,262,091
11	86,135,587
12	29,474,647
13	64,926,012
14	43,864,964
15	30,236,771
16	37,778,627
17	81,291,709
18	37,006,688
19	56,327,553
20	38,185,370
21	66,798,298
22	75,126,679
23	15,285,265
24	32,454,367

Multiplication Table

X	1	2	3	4	5	6	7	8	9	10
1	1	2	3	4	5	6	7	8	9	10
2	2	4	6	8	10	12	14	16	18	20
3	3	6	9	12	15	18	21	24	27	30
4	4	8	12	16	20	24	28	32	36	40
5	5	10	15	20	25	30	35	40	45	50
6	6	12	18	24	30	36	42	48	54	60
7	7	14	21	28	35	42	49	56	63	70
8	8	16	24	32	40	48	56	64	72	80
9	9	18	27	36	45	54	63	72	81	90
10	10	20	30	40	50	60	70	80	90	100

Pg 27

X	4	5	6
6	24	30	36
5	20	25	30
4	16	20	24
3	12	15	18
2	8	10	12

1.

X	0	6	8	4	9
5	0	30	40	20	45
4	0	24	32	16	36
3	0	18	24	12	27

2.

X	2	3	4	5	6
10	20	30	40	50	60
11	22	33	44	55	66
12	24	36	48	60	72

3.

X	5	4	3
6	30	24	18
5	25	20	15
4	20	16	12
3	15	12	9
2	10	8	6

4.

Pg 28		Pg 29		Pg 30	
No.	Answer	No.	Answer	No.	Answer
1	260	1	1,968	1	735
2	147	2	3,168	2	1,536
3	108	3	432	3	1,944
4	552	4	1,944	4	3,216
5	456	5	2,088	5	5,525
6	392	6	1,036	6	3,404
7	116	7	935	7	3,354
8	160	8	2,046	8	1,015
9	476	9	1,656	9	3,196
10	747	10	288	10	1,800
				11	2,916
				12	5,568
				13	2,666
				14	8,740
				15	1,638
				16	7,200
				17	1,260
				18	6,566
				19	2,128
				20	3,705

Pg 31		Pg 32		Pg 33	
No.	Answer	No.	Answer	No.	Answer
1	42	1	7,383	1	25,532
2	640	2	4,921	2	28,896
3	57	3	22,016	3	36,096
4	72	4	16,524	4	11,713
		5	15,200	5	41,724
		6	24,999	6	40,807
		7	33,418	7	8,668
		8	5,640	8	15,876
		9	21,204	9	9,164
		10	53,952	10	31,178
		11	74,036	11	9,924
		12	37,905	12	18,278
		13	23,970	13	63,264
		14	50,007	14	45,689
		15	47,288	15	37,944
		16	45,045	16	22,743
		17	60,800	17	67,425
		18	57,072	18	14,314
		19	26,826	19	52,500
		20	83,040	20	63,624

Pg 34		Pg 35		Pg 36	
No.	Answer	No.	Answer	No.	Answer
1	3,381	1	77,532	1	31,572
2	956	2	102,915	2	68,740
3	1,536	3	167,684	3	152,875
4	608	4	253,425	4	32,147
		5	90,364	5	134,096
		6	376,467	6	174,801
		7	296,472	7	59,496
		8	230,278	8	226,023
		9	156,581	9	51,940
		10	254,910	10	128,808
		11	238,908	11	465,519
		12	404,247	12	382,932
		13	174,135	13	207,900
		14	606,268	14	641,056
		15	291,712	15	579,198
		16	260,559	16	269,244
		17	718,650	17	196,174
		18	524,688	18	793,945
		19	116,795	19	561,000
		20	488,166	20	885,024

Pg 37		Pg 38		Pg 39	
No.	Answer	No.	Answer	No.	Answer
1	157,680	1	66,794	1	418,284
2	222,221	2	69,689	2	250,355
3	79,530	3	258,937	3	584,168
4	269,346	4	128,853	4	826,428
5	63,784	5	230,955	5	1,660,480
6	120,825	6	130,104	6	1,604,106
7	568,874	7	180,048	7	785,436
8	182,400	8	103,170	8	588,707
9	145,148	9	350,966	9	1,668,172
10	616,710	10	247,648	10	1,940,352
11	110,670	11	140,140	11	3,672,774
12	106,524	12	101,106	12	1,145,224
13	308,355	13	203,109	13	555,182
14	445,060	14	285,950	14	3,315,922
15	473,324	15	104,328	15	3,198,804
		16	273,456	16	2,714,376
		17	180,560	17	4,070,924
		18	193,400	18	5,319,210
		19	87,269	19	5,624,400
		20	582,556	20	6,151,680

Pg 40		Pg 41	
No.	Answer	No.	Answer
1	2,133,216	1	6^4
2	345,555	2	3^3
3	1,143,539	3	5^3
4	1,110,444	4	7^4
5	2,901,440	5	9^5
6	2,880,279	6	8^6
7	1,093,680	7	2^6
8	855,218	8	4^4
9	1,770,131	9	5^3
10	1,327,798	10	6^5
11	4,844,560	11	7^7
12	1,395,384	12	2^3
13	3,455,694	13	3^4
14	630,343	14	9^6
15	1,953,252		
16	1,192,269		
17	5,038,836		
18	782,760		
19	8,052,375		
20	3,588,480		

Copyright © Mometrix Media. You have been licensed one copy of this document for personal use only. Any other reproduction or redistribution is strictly prohibited. All rights reserved.

Pg 42	
No.	Answer
1	9 x 9 x 9 = 729
2	5 x 5 x 5 x 5 x 5 = 3,125
3	8 x 8 x 8 x 8 = 4,096
4	2 x 2 x 2 x 2 x 2 x 2 x 2 x 2 x 2 = 512
5	6 x 6 x 6 x 6 = 1,296
6	4 x 4 x 4 x 4 x 4 = 1,024

Pg 43	
No.	Answer
1	8 x 8 = 64
2	6 x 6 x 6 x 6 x 6 = 7,776
3	7 x 7 x 7 x 7 = 2,401
4	3 x 3 x 3 x 3 x 3 x 3 x 3 x 3 = 6,561
5	4 x 4 x 4 = 64
6	5 x 5 x 5 x 5 x 5 = 3,125

Pg 44	
No.	Answer
1	9 < 16
2	64 > 9
3	16 < 25
4	7,776 > 64
5	27 > 25
6	125 > 49
7	4,096 > 125
8	216 < 729
9	256 < 4,096
10	25 < 81
11	343 > 4
12	256 > 9
13	512 > 16
14	81 < 729
15	36 < 49

Chapter 3 – Division

Pg 47		Pg 48		Pg 49		Pg 50	
No.	**Answer**	**No.**	**Answer**	**No.**	**Answer**	**No.**	**Answer**
1	16 r 1	1	13 r 2	1	8 trips	1	367 r 1
2	7 r 3	2	12 r 3	2	5 days	2	297 r 1
3	12 r 5	3	17 r 2	3	7 apples	3	134
4	45 r 1	4	10 r 2	4	9 cookies		
5	24 r 3	5	39				
6	14 r 2	6	11 r 3				
7	11 r 3	7	14 r 3				
8	33 r 1	8	21 r 1				
		9	15 r 1				
		10	41 r 1				
		11	10 r 7				
		12	12 r 5				

Pg 51		Pg 52		Pg 53	
No.	Answer	No.	Answer	No.	Answer
1	153 r 2	1	65 r 7	1	1,241 r 2
2	32	2	68 r 4	2	569 r 5
3	196	3	129 r 4	3	1,522 r 1
4	139 r 2	4	338 r 1	4	630 r 1
5	90 r 5	5	21 r 2	5	1,325 r 3
6	148 r 4	6	250	6	2,178 r 3
7	188	7	104 r 1	7	632
8	148 r 1	8	122 r 6	8	968 r 1
9	207 r 1	9	37 r 4	9	450 r 4
10	232 r 2	10	275 r 2	10	1,867 r 1
11	111 r 1	11	113 r 1	11	1,142 r 2
12	140 r 6	12	368	12	999 r 3
13	423	13	84 r 12		
14	44 r 2	14	25		
15	204	15	87 r 1		
16	138	16	95 r 3		
17	192 r 2	17	453 r 1		
18	69 r 4	18	83 r 3		
19	75 r 6	19	97 r 2		
20	149 r 3	20	157		

Pg 54		Pg 55		Pg 56	
No.	Answer	No.	Answer	No.	Answer
1	8,447 r 3	1	4540 r 3	1	52 Hours
2	21,624	2	15,337 r 3	2	13 Days
3	7,325 r 1	3	2,160 r 3	3	51 Hours
4	44,652 r 1	4	8,502 r 4	4	119 Sections
5	7,338 r 6	5	32,380 r 1		
6	18,027 r 4	6	10,381 r 4		
7	9,025	7	24,623 r 2		
8	18,327	8	10,136 r 7		
9	19,560 r 1	9	13,302		
10	4,050 r 6	10	8,324 r 3		
11	16,634 r 3	11	3,439 r 5		
12	7,800 r 7	12	14,152 r 4		

Pg 57		Pg 58		Pg 59	
No.	Answer	No.	Answer	No.	Answer
1	21 r 8	1	22 r 5	1	207
2	19 r 10	2	24 r 18	2	148 r 6
3	20 r 9	3	20 r 9	3	137 r 40
4	37 r 5	4	5 r 4	4	111 r 27
5	15 r 24	5	43 r 1	5	226 r 12
6	13 r 24	6	22 r 7	6	259 r 11
7	16 r 16	7	22 r 4	7	213 r 14
8	12 r 9	8	22 r 9	8	291 r 3
9	10 r 53	9	21 r 20	9	203 r 30
10	19 r 19	10	17 r 8	10	118 r 3
		11	10 r 22	11	161 r 17
		12	10 r 26	12	205 r 10
		13	28 r 9		
		14	38 r 5		
		15	23 r 8		
		16	15 r 15		
		17	3		
		18	18 r 3		
		19	7 r 5		
		20	2 r 63		

Pg 60		Pg 61	
No.	Answer	No.	Answer
1	3,229 r 8	1	2,280 r 6
2	2,502 r 29	2	2,268 r 10
3	1,686 r 32	3	1,278 r 3
4	2,237 r 20	4	1,055 r 13
5	2,122 r 17	5	1,357 r 21
6	585 r 7	6	1,189 r 81
7	3,018 r 23	7	459 r 12
8	1,791 r 26	8	1,029 r 5
9	543 r 35	9	1,345 r 15
10	1,057 r 63	10	942 r 87
11	1,128 r 11	11	1,050 r 35
12	1,629 r 9	12	1,113 r 9

Pg 63

$$\frac{1}{4}$$ $=$ $$\frac{2}{8}$$

$$\frac{2}{4}$$ $=$ $$\frac{4}{8}$$

$$\frac{3}{8}$$ $=$ $$\frac{6}{16}$$

$$\frac{5}{8}$$ $=$ $$\frac{10}{16}$$

Pg 64		Pg 65	
No.	Answer	No.	Answer
1	$\dfrac{13}{15}$	1	$\dfrac{21}{73}$
2	$\dfrac{23}{37}$	2	$\dfrac{7}{28}$
3	$\dfrac{49}{80}$	3	$\dfrac{22}{89}$
4	$\dfrac{100}{109}$	4	$\dfrac{20}{146}$
5	$\dfrac{30}{64}$	5	$\dfrac{114}{634}$
6	$\dfrac{14}{21}$	6	$\dfrac{4}{12}$
7	$\dfrac{383}{865}$	7	$\dfrac{283}{759}$
8	$\dfrac{33}{55}$	8	$\dfrac{26}{56}$
9	$\dfrac{10}{13}$	9	$\dfrac{79}{207}$
10	$\dfrac{15}{74}$	10	$\dfrac{13}{49}$
11	$\dfrac{238}{250}$	11	$\dfrac{167}{277}$
12	$\dfrac{7}{94}$	12	$\dfrac{238}{534}$
		13	$\dfrac{66}{88}$
		14	$\dfrac{39}{129}$
		15	$\dfrac{189}{952}$

Pg 66	
No.	**Answer**
1	Tomatoes: $\frac{13}{28}$ Eggplants: $\frac{6}{28}$ Potatoes: $\frac{9}{28}$
2	Blue Jays: $\frac{3}{15}$ Sparrows: $\frac{9}{15}$ Ducks: $\frac{6}{15}$ Eagles: $\frac{1}{15}$
3	Bass: $\frac{2}{17}$ Trout: $\frac{6}{17}$ Guppies: $\frac{5}{17}$ Goldfish: $\frac{4}{17}$
4	Hamburgers: $\frac{15}{76}$ Chicken Wings: $\frac{22}{76}$ Sausages: $\frac{39}{76}$

Pg 67		Pg 68		Pg 69	
No.	Answer	No.	Answer	No.	Answer
1	$\dfrac{5}{5}$	1	3	1	$\dfrac{5}{7}+\dfrac{2}{7}=\dfrac{7}{7}$
2	$\dfrac{3}{3}$	2	12	2	$\dfrac{1}{5}+\dfrac{2}{5}=\dfrac{3}{5}$
3	$\dfrac{8}{8}$	3	3	3	$\dfrac{7}{10}+\dfrac{2}{10}=\dfrac{9}{10}$
4	$\dfrac{3}{3}$	4	4	4	$\dfrac{10}{12}+\dfrac{2}{12}=\dfrac{12}{12}$
5	$\dfrac{7}{7}$	5	4	5	$\dfrac{2}{9}+\dfrac{3}{9}=\dfrac{5}{9}$
6	$\dfrac{9}{9}$	6	6	6	$\dfrac{5}{7}+\dfrac{2}{7}=\dfrac{7}{7}$
7	$\dfrac{4}{4}$	7	1	7	$\dfrac{6}{9}+\dfrac{1}{9}=\dfrac{7}{9}$
8	$\dfrac{6}{6}$	8	5	8	$\dfrac{9}{12}+\dfrac{2}{12}=\dfrac{11}{12}$
9	$\dfrac{6}{6}$	9	3	9	$\dfrac{6}{7}+\dfrac{4}{7}=\dfrac{10}{7}$
		10	5	10	$\dfrac{7}{8}+\dfrac{1}{8}=\dfrac{8}{8}$
		11	7	11	$\dfrac{3}{9}+\dfrac{5}{9}=\dfrac{8}{9}$
		12	18	12	$\dfrac{9}{10}+\dfrac{7}{10}=\dfrac{16}{10}$
		13	12		
		14	5		
		15	5		
		16	9		
		17	4		
		18	5		
		19	9		
		20	6		

Pg 70		Pg 71		Pg 72	
No.	Answer	No.	Answer	No.	Answer
1	$\dfrac{12}{18} - \dfrac{4}{18} = \dfrac{8}{18}$	1	$\dfrac{2}{2}$	1	12
2	$\dfrac{4}{7} - \dfrac{1}{7} = \dfrac{3}{7}$	2	$\dfrac{3}{3}$	2	12
3	$\dfrac{7}{9} - \dfrac{4}{9} = \dfrac{3}{9}$	3	$\dfrac{4}{4}$	3	10
4	$\dfrac{4}{5} - \dfrac{3}{5} = \dfrac{1}{5}$	4	$\dfrac{3}{3}$	4	40
5	$\dfrac{3}{7} - \dfrac{2}{7} = \dfrac{1}{7}$	5	$\dfrac{8}{8}$	5	5
6	$\dfrac{6}{7} - \dfrac{5}{7} = \dfrac{1}{7}$	6	$\dfrac{5}{5}$	6	90
7	$\dfrac{9}{9} - \dfrac{6}{9} = \dfrac{3}{9}$	7	$\dfrac{3}{3}$	7	80
8	$\dfrac{8}{9} - \dfrac{3}{9} = \dfrac{5}{9}$	8	$\dfrac{11}{11}$	8	16
9	$\dfrac{6}{7} - \dfrac{3}{7} = \dfrac{3}{7}$	9	$\dfrac{9}{9}$	9	28
10	$\dfrac{8}{9} - \dfrac{2}{9} = \dfrac{6}{9}$			10	90
11	$\dfrac{5}{6} - \dfrac{2}{6} = \dfrac{3}{6}$			11	14
12	$\dfrac{8}{9} - \dfrac{5}{9} = \dfrac{3}{9}$			12	55
				13	128
				14	15
				15	50
				16	80
				17	12
				18	15
				19	6
				20	16

No.	Pg 73 Answer	No.	Pg 74 Answer
1	$\frac{4}{8} + \frac{1}{8} = \frac{5}{8}$	1	$\frac{10}{20} - \frac{6}{20} = \frac{4}{20}$
2	$\frac{4}{12} + \frac{6}{12} = \frac{10}{12}$	2	$\frac{14}{15} - \frac{12}{15} = \frac{2}{15}$
3	$\frac{6}{21} + \frac{5}{21} = \frac{11}{21}$	3	$\frac{13}{18} - \frac{6}{18} = \frac{7}{18}$
4	$\frac{4}{28} + \frac{21}{28} = \frac{25}{28}$	4	$\frac{35}{40} - \frac{20}{40} = \frac{15}{40}$
5	$\frac{30}{50} + \frac{12}{50} = \frac{42}{50}$	5	$\frac{40}{48} - \frac{29}{48} = \frac{11}{48}$
6	$\frac{6}{24} + \frac{15}{24} = \frac{21}{24}$	6	$\frac{16}{24} - \frac{15}{24} = \frac{1}{24}$
7	$\frac{21}{48} + \frac{16}{48} = \frac{37}{48}$	7	$\frac{36}{49} - \frac{21}{49} = \frac{15}{49}$
8	$\frac{45}{81} + \frac{12}{81} = \frac{57}{81}$	8	$\frac{45}{54} - \frac{29}{54} = \frac{16}{54}$
9	$\frac{9}{36} + \frac{18}{36} = \frac{27}{36}$	9	$\frac{63}{81} - \frac{54}{81} = \frac{9}{81}$
10	$\frac{28}{63} + \frac{5}{63} = \frac{33}{63}$	10	$\frac{54}{63} - \frac{35}{63} = \frac{19}{63}$
11	$\frac{39}{72} + \frac{24}{72} = \frac{63}{72}$	11	$\frac{27}{48} - \frac{24}{48} = \frac{3}{48}$
12	$\frac{17}{56} + \frac{35}{56} = \frac{52}{56}$	12	$\frac{70}{100} - \frac{50}{100} = \frac{20}{100}$

	Pg 75		Pg 76
No.	**Answer**	**No.**	**Answer**
1	$\frac{9}{9} = \frac{2}{3}$	1	$5\frac{10}{12}$
2	$\frac{4}{4} = \frac{1}{3}$	2	$6\frac{4}{9}$
3	$\frac{5}{5} = \frac{4}{7}$	3	$7\frac{4}{5}$
4	$\frac{3}{3} = \frac{3}{8}$	4	$2\frac{20}{23}$
5	$\frac{3}{3} = \frac{5}{7}$	5	$13\frac{6}{8}$
6	$\frac{8}{8} = \frac{2}{5}$	6	$13\frac{10}{15}$
7	$\frac{5}{5} = \frac{2}{5}$	7	$13\frac{30}{39}$
8	$\frac{4}{4} = \frac{4}{9}$	8	$12\frac{9}{10}$
9	$\frac{6}{6} = \frac{2}{5}$	9	$4\frac{5}{19}$
10	$\frac{9}{9} = \frac{1}{3}$	10	$3\frac{5}{8}$
11	$\frac{2}{2} = \frac{4}{7}$	11	$3\frac{6}{16}$
12	$\frac{16}{16} = \frac{1}{2}$	12	$5\frac{4}{6}$
		13	$5\frac{4}{25}$
		14	$11\frac{1}{10}$
		15	$8\frac{27}{44}$

Pg 77		Pg 78	
No.	Answer	No.	Answer
1	$5\frac{5}{10} = 5\frac{1}{2}$	1	$\frac{13}{3}$
2	$9\frac{9}{12} = 9\frac{3}{4}$	2	$\frac{38}{4}$
3	$9\frac{6}{18} = 9\frac{1}{3}$	3	$\frac{13}{2}$
4	$8\frac{4}{8} = 8\frac{1}{2}$	4	$\frac{32}{5}$
5	$12\frac{12}{24} = 12\frac{1}{2}$	5	$\frac{95}{10}$
6	$15\frac{18}{36} = 15\frac{1}{2}$	6	$\frac{21}{5}$
7	$11\frac{21}{56} = 11\frac{3}{8}$	7	$\frac{25}{7}$
8	$14\frac{45}{81} = 14\frac{5}{9}$	8	$\frac{14}{3}$
9	$3\frac{8}{16} = 3\frac{1}{2}$	9	$\frac{26}{5}$
10	$12\frac{4}{12} = 12\frac{1}{3}$	10	$\frac{30}{3}$
11	$8\frac{14}{28} = 8\frac{1}{2}$	11	$\frac{27}{5}$
12	$12\frac{6}{9} = 12\frac{2}{3}$	12	$\frac{18}{8}$
13	$39\frac{28}{42} = 39\frac{2}{3}$	13	$\frac{52}{5}$
14	$18\frac{18}{63} = 18\frac{2}{7}$	14	$\frac{27}{3}$
15	$25\frac{12}{21} = 25\frac{4}{7}$	15	$\frac{69}{11}$
16	$11\frac{20}{50} = 11\frac{2}{5}$	16	$\frac{16}{3}$
		17	$\frac{37}{22}$
		18	$\frac{24}{9}$
		19	$\frac{34}{4}$
		20	$\frac{32}{3}$

Pg 79	
No.	**Answer**
1	7
2	4
3	3
4	9
5	8
6	31
7	5
8	42
9	$2\frac{3}{6}$
10	$2\frac{2}{4}$
11	$3\frac{1}{2}$
12	$2\frac{3}{8}$
13	$5\frac{3}{4}$
14	$8\frac{2}{3}$
15	$5\frac{5}{9}$
16	$5\frac{6}{8}$

Chapter 5 – Decimals

Pg 81		Pg 82		Pg 83		Pg 84	
No.	**Answer**	**No.**	**Answer**	**No.**	**Answer**	**No.**	**Answer**
1	10.83	1	19.44	1	40.365	1	971.2
2	11.55	2	17.82	2	16.728	2	522.16
3	17.01	3	18.61	3	108.352	3	233.49
4	74.83	4	22.83	4	13.774	4	480.18
5	71.38	5	264.57	5	68.174	5	1,535.15
6	71.22	6	85.62	6	131.437	6	856.17
		7	93.31	7	109.184	7	839.27
		8	115.88	8	116.236	8	829.72
		9	1,000.77	9	77.166	9	1,019.78

Pg 85		Pg 86	
No.	Answer	No.	Answer
1	points: 75.4 rebounds: 16.2	1	165.93
2	18.5	2	130.62
3	19.55	3	337.26
4	40.34	4	443.47
		5	898.79
		6	1,328.24
		7	913.05
		8	1,676.61
		9	98.011
		10	47.257
		11	134.537
		12	110.116
		13	752.03
		14	1,591.924
		15	1,292.80
		16	675.154
		17	1,161.326
		18	1,130.321
		19	1,107.368
		20	1,526.574

Pg 87		Pg 88		Pg 89		Pg 90	
No.	Answer	No.	Answer	No.	Answer	No.	Answer
1	2,292.203	1	8,947.33	1	4.55	1	49.97
2	1,024.508	2	14,437.96	2	13.45	2	27.68
3	2,369.367	3	10,098.36	3	27.4	3	13.89
4	1,589.946	4	9,065.53	4	559.93	4	15.96
5	1,602.404	5	20,055.64	5	88.65	5	1.17
6	2,443.596	6	14,216.45	6	298.91	6	30.6
7	2,241.336	7	12,316.47			7	18.17
8	1,953.052	8	8,814.81			8	46.75
9	1,862.583	9	10,754.98			9	17.56
10	2,328.303	10	13,061.62				
11	1,192.89	11	10,903.89				
12	2,315.809	12	11,889.87				
13	3,393.375	13	23,148.84				
14	2,686.997	14	12,299.29				
15	2,241.406	15	10,762.47				
16	2,921.589	16	23,018.72				

Pg 91		Pg 92		Pg 93		Pg 94	
No.	Answer	No.	Answer	No.	Answer	No.	Answer
1	592.45	1	79.312	1	49.33	1	883.23
2	802.22	2	36.252	2	326.39	2	2,100.45
3	293.5	3	55.411	3	105.26	3	4,459.81
4	37.64	4	60.407	4	123.73	4	2,713.83
5	112.21	5	11.221	5	241.84	5	5,062.25
6	466.93	6	338.301	6	341.48	6	7,294.40
7	499.62	7	16.151	7	347.08	7	5,944.50
8	103.94	8	6.905	8	169.62	8	1,416.89
9	279.49	9	579.732	9	534.35	9	2,339.55
				10	465.36	10	4,778.22
				11	87.14	11	2,424.61
				12	33.44	12	1,172.31
				13	44.791	13	452.891
				14	20.014	14	632.574
				15	13.269	15	626.454
				16	5.9	16	316.231
				17	21.28	17	94.845
				18	36.574	18	202.634
				19	42.545	19	153.408
				20	25.487	20	561.034

Pg 95		Pg 96		Pg 97		Pg 98	
No.	Answer	No.	Answer	No.	Answer	No.	Answer
1	17.3123	1	1.35	1	$152.40	1	$519.58
2	39.8811	2	26.82	2	$328.14	2	$333.97
3	21.4554	3	53.96	3	$387.76	3	$777.29
4	45.6271	4	2.41	4	$227.07	4	$642.55
5	164.069			5	$447.00	5	$928.53
6	168.894			6	$1,433.61	6	$1,528.24
7	20.514			7	$585.61	7	$1,213.41
8	109.208			8	$1,281.75	8	$1,605.84
9	10,213.10			9	$889.47	9	$702.13
10	1,588.44			10	$1,343.92	10	$1,236.92
11	6,203.53			11	$771.90	11	$1,142.83
12	5.35945			12	$1,076.38	12	$978.09
13	2,176.26			13	$1,452.60	13	$2,496.52
14	202.851			14	$1,132.89	14	$2,007.13
15	2.03419			15	$1,109.55	15	$2,701.26
16	12.2159			16	$882.25	16	$2,751.54
17	74,083.40					17	1,364.77
18	20,618.30					18	$1,139.83
19	13,601.50					19	$1,405.49
20	1,078.77					20	$1,875.55

Pg 99		Pg 100		Pg 101		Pg 102	
No.	Answer	No.	Answer	No.	Answer	No.	Answer
1	$2.38	1	$167.57	1	53.12	1	22.737
2	$3.35	2	$235.72	2	9.57	2	5.891
3	$1.85	3	$221.39	3	29.48	3	4.446
4	$2.47	4	$205.16	4	21.24	4	34.368
5	$5.31	5	$335.66	5	13.05	5	19.032
6	$1.79	6	$685.64	6	56.95	6	27.36
7	$3.82	7	$141.12	7	13.23	7	35.336
8	$4.63	8	$65.73	8	60.76	8	1,440.60
9	$2.86	9	$213.18	9	44.66	9	8.2917
10	$2.14	10	$508.08	10	77.9	10	194.88
11	$1.75	11	$62.57	11	65.12	11	.24153
12	$4.22	12	$671.71	12	33.63	12	995.9
13	$59.09	13	$275.12	13	30.38	13	32.074
14	$104.35	14	$488.63	14	10.75	14	293.26
15	$76.62	15	$34.40	15	33.93	15	6.6744
16	$222.33	16	$524.21			16	185.52
17	$451.09	17	$212.65			17	2.058
18	$321.63	18	$175.49			18	223.29
19	$441.51	19	$248.53			19	5,603.40
20	$82.86	20	$216.79			20	4.0736
						21	31.524
						22	395.34
						23	26.978
						24	19.91
						25	442.96

Pg 103		Pg 104	
No.	Answer	No.	Answer
1	124.576	1	938.448
2	14.5497	2	357.7665
3	1,656.86	3	449.709
4	167.678	4	1.831536
5	42.526	5	5696.46
6	14.1327	6	1,242.448
7	340.548	7	318.8694
8	110.451	8	304.3408
9	927.5	9	1,371.806
10	24.2934	10	404.9125
11	7303.12	11	248.5998
12	1,762.18	12	27,895.43
13	360.549	13	86.8795
14	509.819	14	185.8618
15	270.338	15	257.2271
16	262.145	16	54,917.25
17	1,653.75	17	624.9639
18	78.4101	18	6,041.386
19	55.062	19	107.1348
20	192.576	20	41,661.18
21	8,360.52		
22	8,045.73		
23	35.1978		
24	27.6216		
25	745.129		

Chapter 6 – Geometry

No.	Pg 108 Answer	No.	Pg 109 Answer
1	74 x 74 = 5,476 in.^{2}	1	11in. x 6in. ÷ 2 = 33 in.^{2}
2	134ft. x 749ft. = 100,366 ft.^{2}	2	12ft. x 17ft. ÷ 2 = 102 ft.^{2}
3	205in. x 205in. = 42,025 in.^{2}	3	5in. x 14in. ÷ 2 = 35 in.^{2}
4	299ft. x 436ft. = 130,364 ft.^{2}	4	75in. x 46in. ÷ 2 =1,72 5in.^{2}
5	637in. x 637in. = 405,769 in.^{2}	5	94in. x 89in. ÷ 2 = 4,183 in.^{2}
6	507yd. x 1,262yd. = 639,834 yd.^{2}	6	112ft. x 156ft. ÷ 2 = 8,736 ft.^{2}

No.	Pg 110 Answer	No.	Pg 111 Answer
1	6 x 6 = 36 ft.^{2}	1	6 + 9 x 6 ÷ 2 = 45 yds.^{2}
2	13 x 5 = 65 in.^{2}	2	24 + 16 x 8 ÷ 2 = 160 ft.^{2}
3	15 x 17 = 255 ft.^{2}	3	20 + 32 x 12 ÷ 2 = 312 in.^{2}
4	75 x 45 = 3,375 ft.^{2}	4	55 + 110 x 40 ÷ 2 = 3,300 ft.^{2}
5	136 x 115 = 15,640 in.^{2}	5	136 + 175 x 212 ÷ 2 = 32,966 in.^{2}
6	563 x 599 = 337,237 ft.^{2}	6	250 + 210 x 88 ÷ 2 = 20,240 in.^{2}

No.	Pg 112 Answer	No.	Pg 113 Answer
1	55 + 36 + 42 + 67 = 197 yd.	1	12 + 4 + 4 + 6 + 8 + 10 = 44 yd.
2	125 + 89 + 89 + 125 = 428 ft.	2	4 + 13 + 1 + 12 + 15 = 45 ft.
3	123 + 215 + 107 + 324 = 769 in.	3	88 + 200 + 96 + 88 + 105 + 88 + 411 = 1,076 in.
4	75 + 347 + 62 + 289 +101 = 874 ft.	4	8 + 8 + 8 + 8 + 8 + 8 + 8 + 8 = 64 ft.
5	572 + 635 + 468 = 1,675 in.	5	20 + 20 + 5 + 15 + 15 + 5 = 80 in.
6	917 + 234 + 705 + 917 = 2,773 yd.	6	35 + 4 + 17 + 20 + 19 + 15 + 4 = 114 in.
		7	60 + 55 + 34 + 27 + 10 = 186 ft.
		8	7 + 18 + 19 + 7 + 22 + 8 + 23 = 104 in.
		9	100 + 100 + 25 + 25 + 27 + 50 + 25 = 352 yd.

Pg 114	
No.	Answer
1	vertex- 1, ray- 2, point- 3
2	vertex-1, line segment-2, point -5
3	line-1, ray-2, point-2
4	line-1, ray-2, vertex-1, point-2
5	ray-3, vertex-2, point-4
6	ray-1, line segment-1, vertex-1, point-4
7	ray- 3, vertex-2, point-4
8	ray-2, line-2, point-2

Pg 115			
No.	Answer		
1	Angle: ABC	Vertex: B	Rays: AB, CB
2	Angle: 123	Vertex: 2	Rays: 12, 23
3	Angle: QRS	Vertex: R	Rays: SR, QR
4	Angle: XYZ	Vertex: Y	Rays: XY, YZ
5	Angle: 456	Vertex: 5	Rays: 45, 56
6	Angle: EFG	Vertex: F	Rays: EF, EG
7	Angle: MNO	Vertex: N	Rays: MN, NO
8	Angle: 678	Vertex: 7	Rays: 67, 78
9	Angle: DEF	Vertex: E	Rays: FE, DE
10	Angle: 789	Vertex: 8	Rays: 78, 89
11	Angle: 012	Vertex: 1	Rays: 01, 12
12	Angle: UVW	Vertex: V	Rays: UV, VW

Pg 117

1. Pyramid
   a. 4
   b.6
   c. 4

2. Cylinder
   a. 0
   b. 2
   c. 3

3. Cube
   a. 8
   b. 12
   c. 6

Pg 118

1. Cone
   a. 1
   b. 1
   c. 2

2. Cuboid
   a. 8
   b. 12
   c. 6

3. Pyramid
   a. 5
   b. 8
   c. 5

Pg 120			
No.	Answer		
1	Circle: A	Radius: AB, AC, AD	Diameter: BC
2	Circle: E	Radius: EF, EH, EG	Diameter: FG
3	Circle: X	Radius: XW, XZ, XY	Diameter: WY
4	Circle: R	Radius: RQ, RS,RT	Diameter: QT
5	Circle: M	Radius: ML, MN, MO	Diameter: LO
6	Circle: X	Radius: XR, XA, XP	Diameter: AR

Pg 121		Pg 122	
No.	Answer	No.	Answer
1	18 ÷ 2 = 9 cm.	1	12 x 2 = 24 in.
2	36 ÷ 2 = 18 in.	2	29 x 2 = 58 cm.
3	112 ÷ 2 = 56 ft.	3	89 x 2 = 178 ft.
4	388 ÷ 2 = 194 in.	4	113 x 2 = 226 cm.
5	956 ÷ 2 = 478 ft.	5	624 x 2 = 1,24 in.
6	3,624 ÷ 2 = 1,812 cm.	6	2,935x 2 = 5,870 ft.

Pg 123	
No.	Answer
1	345.4 in.
2	226.08 cm.
3	942 ft.
4	120.89 ft.
5	3,337.192 in.
6	21.64716 cm.

Pg 126		Pg 127	
No.	**Answer**	**No.**	**Answer**
1	Game 5	1	60
2	Game 1	2	35
3	52 Goals	3	45
4	4 Goals	4	30
5	7 Goals	5	45
6	16 Goals	6	50
7	25 Goals	7	65
8	Games 2 and 8	8	25
		9	40
		10	20
		11	25
		12	5
		13	25
		14	5
		15	20
		16	30
		17	45
		18	10

Pg 128

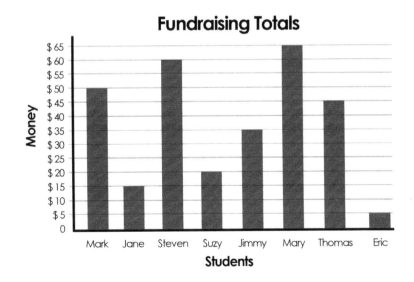

Pg 128	
No.	Answer
1	$45
2	$20
3	$15
4	$35
5	$50
6	$60
7	$65
8	$5
9	$55
10	$15
11	$15
12	$45
13	$45
14	$30

Pg 129	
No.	Answer
1	2012
2	2011
3	85 degrees
4	50 degrees
5	55 degrees
6	Feb
7	July
8	5 degrees
9	90 degrees
10	60 degrees
11	55 degrees
12	10 degrees
13	Stayed the same
14	2011

Pg 130

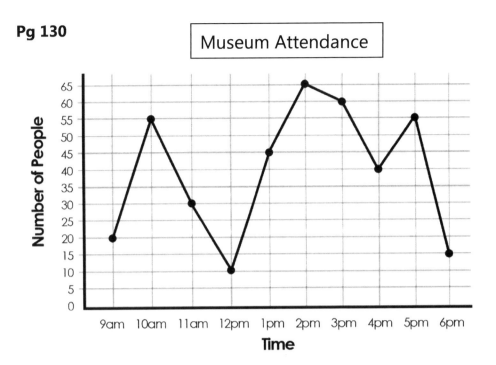

Museum Attendance

Pg 130	
No.	**Answer**
1	2pm
2	12pm
3	10
4	20
5	40
6	25
7	20
8	40
9	12pm - 1pm
10	5pm - 6pm

Pg 131	
No.	Answer
1	A10, C10, C7, E7
2	E10, I10, F7, H7
3	J10, J8, O10, O8
4	Q7, S10, T7
5	A6, A4, B4, B3, D3, D6
6	B2, B1, E5, E2, G5, G1
7	H6, H5, I7, I4, J7, J4, K6, K5
8	I3, I1, L3, O1
9	L7, L4, O5, O4, P7, P6, S6, S5
10	P2, Q4, Q1, S4, S1, T2

Pg 132

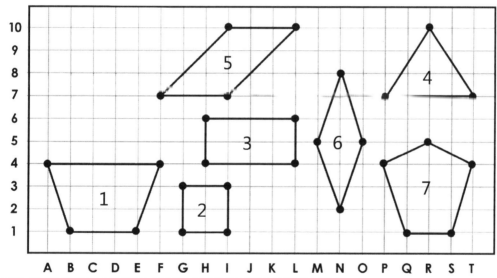

Pg 132	
No.	Answer
1	trapezoid
2	square
3	rectangle
4	triangle
5	parallelogram
6	rhombus
7	pentagon

Pg 133		Pg 135	
No.	Answer	No.	Answer
1	Art	1	Tennis shoes
2	Math	2	Tennis shoes
3	Science	3	Tennis shoes
4	Reading	4	Boots
5	Puppies	5	Sandals
6	Fish	6	Tennis shoes
7	Kittens	7	Boots
8	Gerbil	8	Boots
		9	Boots
		10	Sandals

Pg 136

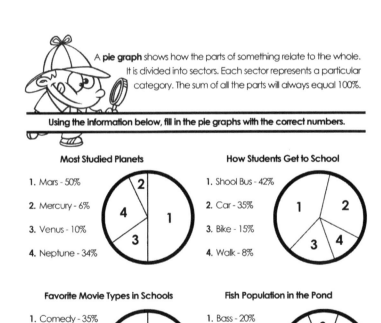

A **pie graph** shows how the parts of something relate to the whole. It is divided into sectors. Each sector represents a particular category. The sum of all the parts will always equal 100%.

Using the information below, fill in the pie graphs with the correct numbers.

Most Studied Planets

1. Mars - 50%
2. Mercury - 6%
3. Venus - 10%
4. Neptune - 34%

How Students Get to School

1. Shool Bus - 42%
2. Car - 35%
3. Bike - 15%
4. Walk - 8%

Favorite Movie Types in Schools

1. Comedy - 35%
2. Action - 18%
3. Drama - 8%
4. Animation - 24%
5. Science Fiction - 15%

Fish Population in the Pond

1. Bass - 20%
2. Catfish - 27%
3. Trout - 14%
4. Guppies - 32%
5. Turtles - 7%

Practice Test Answers

Practice Test #1

Answers and Explanations

1. A: When expressions have braces, brackets, parentheses, begin on the inside and work out. Always work from left to right.

divide 4 by 2	$\{5 \times [9 - (4 \div 2) - 5]\} + 11 =$
subtract 2 from 9	$\{5 \times [9 - 2 - 5]\} + 11 =$
subtract 5 from 7	$\{5 \times [7 - 5]\} + 11 =$
multiply 5 by 2	$\{5 \times 2\} + 11 =$
add 10 and 11	$10 + 11 =$
	21

2. C: When subtraction comes before division, it must be placed in parentheses. The phrase "subtract *4* from *18*" means the same as "*18* minus *4*."

3. C: The first seven terms of the sequence "add *2*" are *0, 2, 4, 6, 8, 10, 12* and the first seven terms of the sequence "add *6*" are *0, 6, 12, 18, 20, 24, 30, 36.* Each of the terms in the "add *6*" sequence is three times the corresponding term in the "add *2*" sequence.

"add *2*" sequence	"add *2*" sequence times *3*	"add *6*" sequence

0	$0 \times 3 = 0$	0
2	$2 \times 3 = 6$	6
4	$4 \times 3 = 12$	12
6	$6 \times 3 = 18$	18
8	$8 \times 3 = 24$	24
10	$10 \times 3 = 30$	30
12	$12 \times 3 = 36$	36

4. A: $100 \times 50 = 5000$, so the *5* would be in the thousands place.

5. B: Four thousand is written *4,000*. Count the zeros to find the exponent.

6. C: The exponent *5* means there are *5* zeros in the answer.

7. A: *5* is in the thousands place, *4* is in the hundreds place, *8* is in the tens place, *2* is in the ones place, *6* is in the hundredths place, and *1* is in the thousandths place.

8. D: 0×10 means a *0* must be written in the tens place.

9. B: All the other numbers are smaller than *21,561.72*, but *21,571.72* is *10* more than *21,561.72*.

10. C: To round to the thousands place, look at the digit to the right (in the hundreds place). If that digit is *4* or less, leave the digit in the thousands place; if that digit is *5* or more, add one to the digit in the thousands place.

11. B: Multiply *4* times *5,349*. Then multiply *20* times *5,349*. Finally, add the two numbers together.

$$
\begin{array}{r}
5,349 \\
\times\ 24 \\
\hline
21,396 \\
+106,980 \\
\hline
128,376
\end{array}
$$

12. D: Find the number of times *28* goes into *35*; record this result (*1*) above the *5*. Subtract *28* (*28* × *1*) from *35* and bring down the *8*. Find the number of times *28* goes into *78*, record this result (*2*) above the *8*. Subtract *56* (*28* × *2*) from *78* and bring down the *4*. Find the number of times *28* goes into *224*, record this result (*8*) above the *4*. Subtract *224* (*28* × *8*) from *224*.

$$
\begin{array}{r}
128 \\
28{\overline{\smash{\big)}\,3584}} \\
-28 \\
\hline
78 \\
-56 \\
\hline
224 \\
-224 \\
\hline
0
\end{array}
$$

13. B: Since *3* items are being purchased and each costs *$3.99*, these two numbers must be multiplied. Choice A shows $3 \times 4 - 3 \times 0.01 = 3 \times (4 - 0.01) = 3 \times 3.99$. Choice C shows $3 \times 3 + 3 \times 0.9 + 3 \times 0.09 = 3 \times (3 + 0.9 + 0.09) = 3 \times 3.99$. Choice D shows $3.99 + 3.99 + 3.99 = 3 \times 3.99$. Only choice B shows a different operation: division.

14. C: To add fractions with unlike denominators, a least common denominator must be found. For these two fractions, the LCD is $5 \times 11 = 55$. Both the numerator and denominator of the first fraction must be multiplied by *11* $\left(\frac{3 \times 11}{5 \times 11} = \frac{33}{55}\right)$) and both the numerator and denominator of the second fraction must be multiplied by *5* $\left(\frac{8 \times 5}{11 \times 5} = \frac{40}{55}\right)$). Now the fractions can be added by finding the sum of the two numerators $\left(\frac{33}{55} + \frac{40}{55} = \frac{73}{55}\right)$). Because this is an improper fraction, the fraction must be rewritten as a whole number and a proper fraction. *55* goes into *73* once (so *1* is the whole number) and the remainder is $73 - 55 = 18$ (so the proper fraction is $\frac{18}{55}$).

15. B: Find the fraction of pizza left over from each pizza.

PIZZA:	pepperoni	cheese	sausage	ham and pineapple	vegetable
eaten:	$\frac{6}{8}$	$\frac{9}{12}$	$\frac{6}{6}$	$\frac{4}{8}$	$\frac{1}{6}$
left over:	$\frac{2}{8} = \frac{1}{4}$	$\frac{3}{12} = \frac{1}{4}$	0	$\frac{4}{8} = \frac{1}{2}$	$\frac{5}{6}$

Find the least common denominator.
$$\frac{1}{4} + \frac{1}{4} + \frac{1}{2} + \frac{5}{6} = \frac{1 \times 3}{4 \times 3} + \frac{1 \times 3}{4 \times 3} + \frac{1 \times 6}{2 \times 6} + \frac{5 \times 2}{6 \times 2} = \frac{3}{12} + \frac{3}{12} + \frac{16}{12} + \frac{10}{12}$$
Add the four fractions together.
$$\frac{3}{12} + \frac{3}{12} + \frac{16}{12} + \frac{10}{12} = \frac{22}{12}$$
Find the mixed number.
$$\frac{22}{12} = 1\frac{10}{12} = 1\frac{10 \div 2}{12 \div 2} = 1\frac{5}{6}$$

16. C: First, find the least common denominator: $\frac{4 \times 16}{5 \times 16} - \frac{1 \times 5}{16 \times 5} = \frac{64}{80} - \frac{5}{80}$ then subtract the numerators: $\frac{64}{80} - \frac{5}{80} = \frac{59}{80}$ To find where this answer lies on the number line, consider that $0 = \frac{0}{80}$, $\frac{1}{4} = \frac{20}{80}$, $\frac{1}{2} = \frac{40}{80}$, $\frac{3}{4} = \frac{60}{80}$ and $1 = \frac{80}{80}$. So $\frac{59}{80}$ is between $\frac{40}{80} = \frac{1}{2}$ and $\frac{60}{80} = \frac{3}{4}$

17. D: The answer is found by dividing the number of cans by the number of dogs: $\frac{5 \text{ cans}}{4 \text{ dogs}}$. The fraction is improper, so rewrite it as a mixed number: 4 goes into 5 once (so the whole number is *1*) and the remainder is $5 - 4 = 1$ (so the numerator of the fraction is *1*).

18. B: The answer is found by dividing the number of quarts by the number of girls: $\frac{4 \text{ quarts}}{7 \text{ girls}}$.

19. B: Henry ate $\frac{3}{4}$ of a candy bar for 5 days. To find the total number of candy bars, multiply $\frac{3}{4} \times 5 = 3 \times 5 \div 4 = \frac{15}{4} = 3\frac{3}{4}$.

Monday   Tuesday   Wednesday   Thursday   Friday

20. A:

$\frac{3}{8}$ in

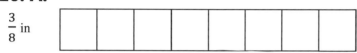

3 in

Each tile has an area of $\frac{3}{8} \times \frac{3}{8} = (3 \times 3) \div (8 \times 8) = \frac{9}{64}$ in². There are 8 tiles, so the area of the rectangle is $\frac{9}{64} \times 8 = 9 \times 8 \div 64 = \frac{72}{64} = \frac{9}{8} = 1\frac{1}{8}$ in².

Multiplying the length and the width gives the same answer: $\frac{3}{8} \times 3 = 3 \times 3 \div 8 = \frac{9}{8} = 1\frac{1}{8}$ in².

21. D: Since 24 is larger than 15, the answer to *487,956 × 24* must be larger than the answer to *487,956 × 15*.

22. A: When a fraction is multiplied by *0*, the result is zero. When a fraction is multiplied by *1*, the result is the same fraction. When a fraction is multiplied by a fraction between *0* and *1*, the result is between *0* and the same fraction. When a fraction is multiplied by a fraction larger than *1*, the result is larger than the fraction.

23. D: The area is found by multiplying $20\frac{1}{2} \times 36\frac{1}{2} = \frac{41}{2} \times \frac{73}{2} = \frac{2993}{4} = 748\frac{1}{4}$ in².

24. D: All *5* of the pieces must be cut into *3*, creating *15* equal sections. The answer can be verified using multiplication: $\frac{1}{15} \times 3 = 1 \times 3 \div 15 = \frac{3}{15} = \frac{1}{5}$.

25. C: Choices A and B are based on division, with the correct divisor and dividend. Choice D is based on multiplication, the opposite of division, using the given numbers as one of the factors and the product. Only choice C is incorrect because it has the divisor and dividend confused.

26. A: Each family member is taking $\frac{1}{5}$ of the $\frac{1}{2}$ gallon. That divides the whole gallon into 10 parts, so each family member gets $\frac{1}{10}$ of a gallon. The answer can be verified using multiplication: $\frac{1}{10} \times 5 = 1 \times 5 \div 10 = \frac{5}{10} = \frac{1}{2}$.

27. D: To convert from feet to inches, multiply by the factor $\frac{12\,in}{1\,ft}$:
$15\,ft \times \frac{12\,in}{1\,ft} = 180$ in.

28. C: $\$12.50 \times \frac{1\,ft}{\$2.50} \times \frac{12\,in}{1\,ft} = (12.50 \div 2.50) \times 12\ in = 5 \times 12\ in = 60$ in.

29. B: First, find the total amount of milk in the cartons: $4 \times \frac{1}{4} + 3 \times \frac{1}{2} + 2 \times \frac{3}{4} = 1 + \frac{3}{2} + \frac{6}{4} = \frac{2}{2} + \frac{3}{2} + \frac{3}{2} = \frac{8}{2} = 4$ cartons of milk. Then, divide the amount of milk by the number of cartons: $\frac{4}{9}$.

30. B: A unit cube must have side lengths of 1 unit. Since choice B has side lengths of 2 mm, it cannot be a unit cube.

31. D: There are 18 unit cubes on the front of the box, so the middle and the back will also have 18 unit cubes each. $18 \times 3 = 54$ unit cubes.

32. A: To find the volume, draw the unit cubes in to see that there are 5 across, 2 deep, and 3 up and down. Then count the number of cubes. There are 15 on the front and a matching 15 on the back: $15 + 15 = 30$ cubic inches.

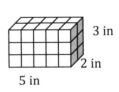

3 in

2 in

5 in

33. D: Choices A, finding the number of unit cubes that fit inside the solid, B, multiplying the side lengths, and C, multiplying the area of the base times the height, will give the same result: the volume. Choice D, adding the side lengths will not result in the volume.

34. A: $V = B \times h = 50 \times 3 = 150$ cubic centimeters.

35. C: $V = l \times w \times h = 6 \times 4 \times 10 = 240$ cubic inches.

36. C: $V_{top} = l \times w \times h = 1 \times 1 \times 9 = 9$ and $V_{bottom} = l \times w \times h = 8 \times 3 \times 5 = 120$. Volume is additive, so adding the two individual volumes will result in the total volume: $V_{top} + V_{bottom} = 9 + 120 = 129$ cubic inches.

37. B: $V_{top} = l \times w \times h = 7 \times 7 \times 7 = 343$ and $V_{bottom} = l \times w \times h = 21 \times 7 \times 7 = 1029$. Volume is additive, so adding the two individual volumes will result in the total volume: $V_{top} + V_{bottom} = 343 + 1029 = 1372$ cubic centimeters.

38. A: Point A is located at $(4,2)$, the point four units to the right of the origin and two units above the origin.

39. D: The school is located six units to the right of the origin and four units above the origin, at $(6,4)$.

40. D: Find the ordered pair with 5 as the x-value that lies on the line. The y-value of that ordered pair is 275.

41. B: A trapezoid has only one pair of parallel sides. A square, a rectangle, and a rhombus all have two pairs of parallel sides.

42. A: All equilateral triangles have three equal sides and three equal angles. The measure of those angles is $60°$, so those angles can only be acute.

Practice Test #2

Answers and Explanations

1. B: Expressions with braces, brackets, parentheses, must be solved from the inside out and are always solved from left to right.

add 3 and 4	${[42 \div (3 + 4) + 8] \times 3 + 8} \div 25 =$
divide 42 by 7	${[42 \div 7 + 8] \times 3 + 8} \div 25 =$
add 6 to 8	${[6 + 8] \times 3 + 8} \div 25 =$
multiply 14 by 3	${14 \times 3 + 8} \div 25 =$
add 42 and 8	${42 + 8} \div 25 =$
divide 50 by 25	$50 \div 25 =$
	2

2. A: The difference between 24 and 6 must be found before the multiplication can be done, so $24 - 6$ must be in parentheses.

3. C: The first seven terms of the sequence "add 5" are $0, 5, 10, 15, 20, 25, 30$ and the first seven terms of the sequence "add 10" are $0, 10, 20, 30, 40, 50, 60$. Each of the terms in the "add 5" sequence is half (divide by 2) the corresponding term in the "add 10" sequence.

"add 10" sequence	"add 10" sequence divided by2	"add 5" sequence
0	$0 \div 2 = 0$	0
10	$10 \div 2 = 5$	5
20	$20 \div 2 = 10$	10
30	$30 \div 2 = 15$	15
40	$40 \div 2 = 20$	20
50	$50 \div 2 = 25$	25
60	$60 \div 2 = 30$	30

4. A: $9,000,000 \div 100 = 90,000$, so the 9 would be in the ten thousands place.

5. B: Seventy thousand is written $70,000$. Count the zeros to find the exponent.

6. D: The exponent 3 means the 2 is three places behind the decimal.

7. C: 9 is in the ten thousands place, 2 is in the thousands place, 4 is in the hundreds place, 0 is in the tens place, 4 is in the ones place, 2 is in the tenths place, and 6 is in the hundredths place. The 0 in the tens place cannot be skipped.

8. B: 0 must hold the tenths place for $0 \times \frac{1}{10}$. $4 \times \frac{1}{100}$ means 4 must be in the second place behind the decimal.

9. A: Choice B is equal to, not less than, 52,468.19 and choices C and D are larger than 52,468.19, but choice A, 52,458.19, is 10 less than 52,468.19.

10. D: To round to the hundredths place, look at the digit to the right (in the thousandths place). If that digit is 4 or less, leave the digit in the hundredths place; if that digit is 5 or more, add one to the digit in the hundredths place.

11. C: Multiply 2 times 4,298. Then multiply 50 times 4,298. Finally, add the two numbers together.

$$
\begin{array}{r}
5{,}349 \\
\times\,24 \\
\hline
8{,}596 \\
+214{,}900 \\
\hline
223{,}496
\end{array}
$$

12. D: Find the number of times 31 goes into 152; record this result (4) above the 2. Subtract 124 (31 × 4) from 152 and bring down the 2. Find the number of times 31 goes into 282; record this result (9) above the 2. Subtract 279 (31 × 9) from 282 and bring down the 1. Find the number of times 31 goes into 31; record this result (1) above the 1. Subtract 31 (31 × 1) from 31.

$$
\begin{array}{r}
491 \\
31)\overline{15221} \\
-124 \\
\hline
282 \\
-279 \\
\hline
31 \\
-31 \\
\hline
0
\end{array}
$$

13. C: Since 4 items are being purchased for $23.96, these two numbers must be divided. Choice A shows $\frac{24}{4} - \frac{0.04}{4} = \frac{24-.04}{4} = \frac{23.96}{4}$. Choice B shows $\frac{20}{4} + \left(\frac{4}{4} - \frac{0.04}{4}\right) = \frac{20}{4} + \left(\frac{4-0.04}{4}\right) = \frac{20+(4-.04)}{4} = \frac{20+(3.96)}{4} = \frac{23.96}{4}$. Choice D shows $23.96 \div 4 = \frac{23.96}{4}$. Only choice C shows a different operation: multiplication.

14. B: To subtract fractions with unlike denominators, a least common denominator must be found. For these two fractions, the LCD is $3 \times 5 = 15$. Both the numerator and denominator of the first fraction must be multiplied by 5 $\left(\frac{2\times5}{3\times5} = \frac{10}{15}\right)$ and both the numerator and denominator of the second fraction must be multiplied by 3 $\left(\frac{1\times3}{5\times3}=\frac{3}{15}\right)$. Now the fractions can be subtracted by finding the difference between the two numerators $\left(\frac{10}{15}-\frac{3}{15}=\frac{7}{15}\right)$.

15. B:
Find the fraction of pie left over from each pie.

PIE:	cherry	first apple	second apple	pecan	first pumpkin	second pumpkin
eaten:	$\frac{5}{10}$	$\frac{7}{8}$	$\frac{9}{10}$	$\frac{6}{8}$	$\frac{6}{8}$	$\frac{12}{12}$
left over:	$\frac{5}{10}=\frac{1}{2}$	$\frac{1}{8}$	$\frac{1}{10}$	$\frac{2}{8}=\frac{1}{4}$	$\frac{2}{8}=\frac{1}{4}$	0

Find the least common denominator.
$$\frac{1}{2}+\frac{1}{8}+\frac{1}{10}+\frac{1}{4}+\frac{1}{4}=\frac{1\times20}{2\times20}+\frac{1\times5}{8\times5}+\frac{1\times4}{10\times4}+\frac{1\times10}{4\times10}+\frac{1\times10}{4\times10}$$
$$=\frac{20}{40}+\frac{5}{40}+\frac{4}{40}+\frac{10}{40}+\frac{10}{40}$$
Add the five fractions together.
$$\frac{20}{40}+\frac{5}{40}+\frac{4}{40}+\frac{10}{40}+\frac{10}{40}=\frac{49}{40}$$
Find the mixed number.
$$\frac{49}{40}=1\frac{9}{40}$$

16. D:
First, find the least common denominator: $\frac{1\times6}{8\times6}+\frac{5\times8}{6\times8}=\frac{6}{48}+\frac{40}{48}$, then add the numerators: $\frac{6}{48}+\frac{40}{48}=\frac{46}{48}=\frac{46\div2}{48\div2}=\frac{23}{24}$. To find where this answer lies on the number line, consider that $0=\frac{0}{24}$, $\frac{1}{4}=\frac{6}{24}$, $\frac{1}{2}=\frac{12}{24}$, $\frac{3}{4}=\frac{18}{24}$, and $1=\frac{24}{24}$. So $\frac{23}{24}$ is between $\frac{18}{24}=\frac{3}{4}$ and $\frac{24}{24}=1$. Alternatively, consider that $\frac{5}{6}=\frac{20}{24}$ is already greater than $\frac{18}{24}=\frac{3}{4}$, so adding any fraction less than $\frac{1}{6}=\frac{4}{24}$ will be between $\frac{18}{24}=\frac{3}{4}$ and $\frac{24}{24}=1$. Since $\frac{1}{8}=\frac{3}{24}$, the answer is between $\frac{18}{24}=\frac{3}{4}$ and $\frac{24}{24}=1$.

17. A: The answer is found by dividing the number of cookies by the number of people: $\frac{3 \text{ cookies}}{9 \text{ people}}$. Don't forget to include Maria in the number of people! Reduce the fraction to find the answer: $\frac{3 \div 3}{9 \div 3} = \frac{1}{3}$ of a cookie for each person.

18. C: The answer is found by subtracting the number of servings eaten from the number of servings total: $5 - 3 = 2$, then dividing that answer by the total number of servings: $\frac{2 \text{ servings left}}{5 \text{ servings total}}$.

19. A: Ana wore $\frac{3}{2}$ pairs of socks each day for 4 days. Multiply these two numbers together to find the number of pairs of socks in the laundry: $\frac{3}{2} \times 4 = 3 \times 4 \div 2 = 12 \div 2 = 6$ pairs.

20. D:

Each tile has an area of $\frac{2}{5} \times \frac{2}{5} = (2 \times 2) \div (5 \times 5) = \frac{4}{25}$ cm^2. There are 10 tiles, so the area of the rectangle is $\frac{4}{25} \times 10 = 4 \times 10 \div 25 = \frac{40}{25} = 1\frac{15}{25} = 1\frac{3}{5}$ cm^2. Multiplying the length and the width gives the same answer: $\frac{2}{5} \times 4 = 2 \times 4 \div 5 = \frac{8}{5} = 1\frac{3}{5}$ cm^2.

21. D: Since 4,500 is smaller than 5,000, the answer to $0.00542 \times 4,500$ must be smaller than the answer to $0.00542 \times 5,000$.

22. D: When a number is multiplied by 0, the result is zero. When a number is multiplied by 1, the result is the same number. When a number is multiplied by a fraction between 0 and 1, the result is between 0 and the same number. When a number is multiplied by a fraction larger than 1, the result is larger than the number.

23. C: The area is found by multiplying $11\frac{1}{2} \times 14\frac{1}{2} = \frac{23}{2} \times \frac{29}{2} = \frac{667}{4} = 166\frac{3}{4}$ in².

24. B: All 12 of the pieces must be cut into 4, creating 48 equal sections. The answer can be verified using multiplication: $\frac{1}{48} \times 4 = 1 \times 4 \div 48 = \frac{4}{48} = \frac{1}{12}$.

25. A: Choices B and C are based on division, with the correct divisor and dividend. Choice D is based on multiplication, the opposite of division, using the given numbers as one of the factors and the product. Only choice A is incorrect because it has the divisor and dividend confused.

26. D: Each runner is running $\frac{1}{8}$ of the $\frac{1}{3}$ mile. That divides a whole mile into 24 parts, so each person runs $\frac{1}{24}$ of a mile. The answer can be verified using multiplication: $\frac{1}{24} \times 8 = 1 \times 8 \div 24 = \frac{8}{24} = \frac{1}{3}$.

27. C: To convert from meters to millimeters, multiply by the factor $\frac{1000 \text{ mm}}{1 \text{ m}}$: $2.6 \text{ m} \times \frac{1000 \text{ mm}}{1 \text{ m}} = 2{,}600 \text{ mm}$.

28. A: $\$20.00 \times \frac{15 \text{ ft}}{\$4.00} \times \frac{1 \text{ yd}}{3 \text{ ft}} = 20 \times 15 \div 4 \div 3 = 300 \div 4 \div 3 = 75 \div 3 = 25$ yd.

29. C: First, find the total amount of water in the bowls: $4 \times \frac{1}{4} + 3 \times \frac{1}{2} + 2 \times \frac{3}{4} + 1 \times 1 = 1 + \frac{3}{2} + \frac{6}{4} + 1 = \frac{2}{2} + \frac{3}{2} + \frac{3}{2} + \frac{2}{2} = \frac{10}{2} = 5$ bowls of water. Then, divide the amount of water by the number of bowls: $\frac{5}{10} = \frac{1}{2}$.

30. B: A unit cube must have side lengths of 1 unit. Since choice A has side lengths of 2 ft, choice C has side lengths of 5 in, and choice D has side lengths of 8 cm, they cannot be unit cubes.

31. C: There are 24 unit cubes on the top of the box, so the bottom will also have 24 unit cubes. $24 \times 2 = 48$ unit cubes.

32. A: To find the volume, draw the unit cubes in to see that there are 4 across, 1 deep, and 2 up and down. Then count the number of cubes. There are 4 on the top and a matching 4 on the bottom: $4 + 4 = 8$ cubic meters.

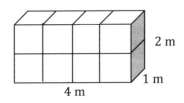

33. A: Choices B, finding the number of unit cubes that fit inside the solid, C, multiplying the area of the base times the height, and D, multiplying the side lengths, will give the same result: the volume. Choice A, adding the side lengths, will not result in the volume.

34. D: $V = B \times h = 121 \times 6 = 726$ cubic inches.

35. D: $V = l \times w \times h = 25 \times 10 \times 15 = 250 \times 15 = 3{,}750$ cubic millimeters.

36. A: $V_{top} = l \times w \times h = 15 \times 6 \times 6 = 90 \times 6 = 540$ and $V_{bottom} = l \times w \times h = 21 \times 8 \times 10 = 21 \times 80 = 1680$. Volume is additive, so adding the two individual volumes will result in the total volume: $V_{top} + V_{bottom} = 540 + 1680 = 2{,}220$ cubic inches.

37. D: $V_{top} = l \times w \times h = 16 \times 8 \times 8 = 128 \times 8 = 1024$ and $V_{bottom} = l \times w \times h = 16 \times 8 \times 8 = 128 \times 8 = 1024$. Volume is additive, so adding the two individual volumes will result in the total volume: $V_{top} + V_{bottom} = 1024 + 1024 = 2048$ cubic inches.

38. B: Point B is located at (3,1), the point three units to the right of the origin and one unit above the origin.

39. A: The mall is located three units directly above the origin, at (0,3).

40. B: Find the ordered pair with 212 as the y-value that lies on the line. The x-value of that ordered pair is 5.

41. B: All isosceles triangles have two equal sides and two equal angles. The equal angles are called base angles and cannot be obtuse. The sum of the three angles is 180° and obtuse angles are greater than 90°. Two obtuse angles would have a sum greater than 180°, so they cannot form a triangle.

42. C: Parallelograms, rhombi, and trapezoids do not necessarily have four right angles. Squares do, so they are rectangles.

Additional Bonus Material

Due to our efforts to try to keep this book to a manageable length, we've created a link that will give you access to all of your additional bonus material.

Please visit http://www.mometrix.com/bonus948/mcag5math to access the information.